P

FRANCIS MARION

The Swamp Fox
of the American Revolution

Louis P. Towles

The Rosen Publishing Group's
PowerPlus Books™
New York

Published in 2002 by The Rosen Publishing Group, Inc.
29 East 21st Street, New York, NY 10010

Copyright © 2002 by The Rosen Publishing Group, Inc.

First Edition

Editor's Note: All quotations have been reproduced as they appeared in the letters and diaries from which they were borrowed. No correction was made to the inconsistent spelling that was common in that time period.

Library of Congress Cataloging-in-Publication Data

Towles, Louis P. (Louis Palmer), 1943–
       Francis Marion : the Swamp Fox of the American Revolution / by Louis P. Towles.
       p. cm. — (The library of American lives and times)
Includes bibliographical references and index.
ISBN 0-8239-5728-4 (lib. bdg.)
1. Marion, Francis, 1732–1795—Juvenile literature. 2. Generals—United States—Biography—Juvenile literature. 3. South Carolina—Militia—Biography—Juvenile literature. 4. United States—History—Revolution, 1775–1783—Biography—Juvenile literature. 5. South Carolina—History—Revolution, 1775–1783—Juvenile literature. [1. Marion, Francis, 1732–1795. 2. Generals. 3. United States—History—Revolution, 1775–1783—Biography.] I. Title. II. Series.
E207.M3 T69 2002
973.3'3'092—dc21

                                                                00–013036

Manufactured in the United States of America

CONTENTS

Preface

Everyday life can be predictable, even boring. People rise, eat, work or play, and then rest before beginning another day. Everyone knows what he or she must do, and how it should be accomplished. People work by rules, and they are comfortable doing it. In a time of crisis, however, when there are no rules or structure, people are often at a loss for what to do next.

Most individuals do not deal easily with the unexpected or the unplanned. Some panic, others react poorly, and most either are disorganized or do nothing at all. They wait for a leader to emerge, someone who can provide order, someone who can tell them what to do, someone like George Washington, or Abraham Lincoln, or the Roosevelts—Theodore and Franklin. Yet not all leaders are as well known as the above. Many are unknowns, people who are drawn to the forefront by

Opposite: This 1973 painting by D. L. Eklund shows Francis Marion leading his men through the swamplands of South Carolina. Marion was known for riding hard through the night to surprise an unsuspecting enemy at dawn.

need—John Smith and William Bradford, Tecumseh and Blackhawk, Daniel Boone and Andrew Jackson, Nathanael Greene and Francis Marion, Stonewall Jackson and Bedford Forrest, and Clara Barton and Martin Luther King Jr.

Of this latter group, Francis Marion is one of the brightest stars, though possibly the least known to people today. He emerged from almost total obscurity and gave his all to the patriot cause in South Carolina during the American Revolution. He performed brilliantly during the latter stages of the conflict as a commander of volunteer troops, or militia. In the process, he sacrificed all that he had in order to assist his countrymen. He retired quietly when the work was done, asking nothing for his service and leaving few records of his activities.

Parson Mason Weems lived from 1759 to 1825. After preaching, he took up book selling, and then writing, to pay the bills.

In the years following Francis Marion's death, his friend, Peter Horry, wrote an account of the departed leader to satisfy friends and to award Marion the credit he never sought in life. Unsure of his abilities as a writer, Horry permitted Parson M. L. Weems, George Washington's first biographer, to edit and publish the work. The result was most unsatisfactory. Weems drastically altered the manuscript to make

This 1795 portrait of George Washington was painted by
Gilbert Stuart. Washington, president from 1789 to 1797, was
sixty-three at the time. Stuart made more than a hundred likenesses
of Washington, grouped in categories named after the first owners of
the original portraits. Because the painting here was purchased by
Samuel Vaughan, Vaughan's name became associated with seventeen
versions where Washington faces to the left, all based on this original.

Marion sound like the South's equivalent to Washington, Weems's hero. Numerous fictional accounts were introduced into the text before it was published, and Horry's account was never returned to him. All that Peter Horry could sadly comment when he read the result was that "all this . . . is the fruitful invention of the Brain of Mr. Weems." In writing to Weems in protest, Horry commented, "Most certainly 'tis not my history, but your romance."

A life story of Francis Marion, a man who shunned publicity, must therefore be written with great care. The Horry-Weems account certainly cannot be avoided, but, as much as possible, other sources should be used first, or to verify Weems. For example, during Marion's stay at Snow Island in 1781, a British officer was captured, blindfolded, and brought to Colonel Marion to be questioned. When the blindfold was removed, the young officer was amazed at Marion's small physical size, the primitive conditions of the camp, and the few roasted potatoes that each soldier had for food. Marion is said to have responded that "we are fortunate on this occasion, entertaining company, to have more than our usual allowance." The officer, when he was returned to Georgetown, was said to have resigned his commission, because men such as Marion's "were not to be subdued." In this very popular and often-repeated tale, the potatoes were probably real, but the fact that Marion released an officer and the officer resigned his commission is very questionable. As a result, this account, although classic, is too suspect to be used by a true historian. Everything considered, it is the conclusion of this author that the Swamp Fox in death is harder to find than when he roamed the swamps of Williamsburg District from 1780 to 1783. Nonetheless, let us go in search of him and see what truths we might uncover from the hiding places of history.

1. The Making of a Man, 1732–1748

Francis Marion, the youngest of six children, was born to Gabriel and Esther Marion in St. Johns Parish of the colony of South Carolina. His birth at Goatfield Plantation, his father's home, possibly in the early winter of 1732, was almost unnoticed. The child, named for his uncle, was unusually small and probably premature, with underdeveloped legs and ankles that made him appear so tiny as to be "easily enough . . . put in a quart pot." Furthermore, as he grew, he was not very attractive. He possessed a large head, a long nose, and a small body. His legs and ankles would bother him throughout his life.

The boy was of French descent. His grandparents, Benjamin and Judith, were French Calvinists, or Huguenots, who had left their native land in the late 1680s. They left because, like other French Protestants, they were gradually being denied their

Opposite: This is an undated portrait of General Francis Marion by an unknown artist. Marion lived from around 1732 to 1795. He became known as the Swamp Fox during the Revolutionary War. He grew up in the swamplands of South Carolina, and later his knowledge of the territory would help him launch surprise attacks against the British.

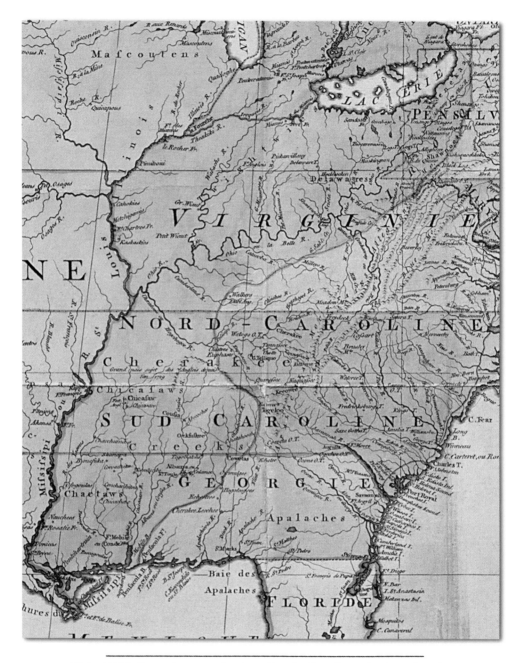

This 1755 French map depicts South Carolina during the time
that Francis Marion was growing up. Starting in the 1600s,
the French and English arrived and took over the land from
the Cherokee Indians, who were native to the area.

freedom of worship. Benjamin and Judith Marion and their eldest children, Esther and Gabriel, arrived in the colony and were naturalized, or given partial citizenship, in 1696. Benjamin first settled his rapidly growing family in the parish of Saint Dennis with other French settlers who did not read or write English. In 1711, he moved to St. Johns Parish, where he and his son Gabriel both acquired land. Benjamin, who spoke little English, wrote his will in French fourteen years later. He died in 1735, three years after Francis, his grandson, was born.

By 1716, Gabriel Marion, Benjamin's eldest son, was married to Esther Cordes, a neighbor also of French descent. The couple produced six children, named Esther, Isaac, Benjamin, Gabriel Jr., Job, and, finally, Francis. Unfortunately Gabriel was not much of a businessman and had difficulty providing for his family. He required help, first from his father and then from Thomas Cordes, his wife's brother. In 1738, Gabriel moved his family to Georgetown, where he could be both a planter and a merchant. He was probably trying to prove himself. Instead he failed within eight years and was forced to sell his land in St. Johns. This led Thomas Cordes to give 1,500 pounds (perhaps $20,000 today) to his sister, Esther Cordes Marion, "to be freely possessed and enjoyed at her own . . . disposal without the control, power or interruption of the said Gabriel Marion, her husband."

Almost nothing is known about Francis Marion's early years. Sources agree that he was a sickly child who was unable to do much. Consequently, little time was devoted to his schooling or to his socialization with others. During this period of his life, he also had little contact with his brothers and sister, who left home in his childhood. Gabriel Jr., or Gabe, and Job returned to St. Johns Parish. Benjamin moved to St. Thomas, Isaac settled on the Little River near the North Carolina border, and Esther was at Winyah Bay. Francis is not known to have developed long-standing friendships, except perhaps with his body servant, Oscar, with whom he was raised. In addition, even though his health improved noticeably after he turned twelve, he was a quiet, thoughtful, passive, and moody youth. In 1748, possibly to help with the family financial crisis, or to seek his fortune elsewhere, he joined the crew of a ship owned by a family friend named Joshua Lockwood. The ship traveled to the West Indies with young Francis on board. Unfortunately, or some might say fortunately for Francis Marion, the small vessel struck a whale on its return voyage and sank. The crew managed to escape in a boat and five of them, including Francis, survived six days at sea by eating a small dog that had been on the ship.

The young man who returned to Georgetown was stronger and wiser for his effort. Already accustomed to hard times, he now added survival to his experiences. Francis realized that the life he had left behind had more to offer than the life at sea he had impulsively chosen.

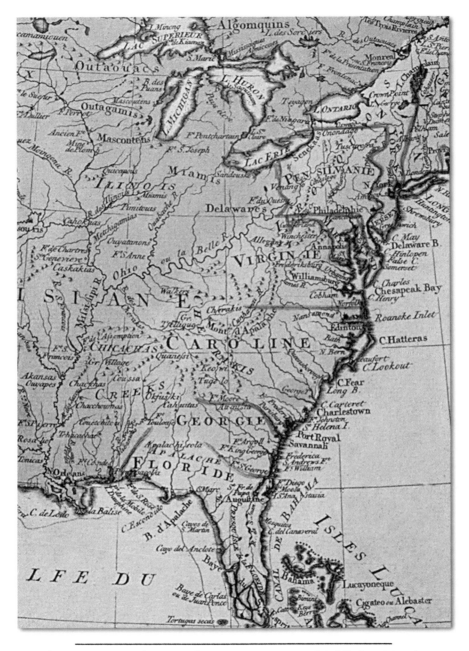

This 1767 French map shows Georgetown, highlighted in the blue oval, where Francis Marion's family moved in 1738. After narrowly escaping death at sea in 1748, Marion returned to Georgetown to help his elderly parents with the family farm.

2. A Planter and a Militiaman, 1748–1761

After his ill-fated voyage, Francis Marion returned to the home of his parents in Georgetown and assisted them in planting his father's land. His parents' health was failing, however, and the responsibility for them and the land fell increasingly upon the growing adolescent. Upon the death of his father in 1751, Francis accepted the invitation of his older brother Gabe to relocate to St. Johns Parish with their mother.

The move was a fortunate one. Esther Marion, who died in 1758, was allowed to live out her remaining years in comparative security with her family around her. She and Francis enjoyed the companionship of Gabe's young children—Gabriel III, Robert, Benjamin, and Catherine. Francis formed a partnership with his brother and farmed an adjacent piece of land. In 1759, Gabe and his wife, Catherine, moved to Belle Isle Plantation in St. Stephens Parish. Francis then worked with his brother Job, who remained in St. Johns. In 1763, he petitioned for and obtained land of his own next to Job's. Ten years later he acquired a small plantation,

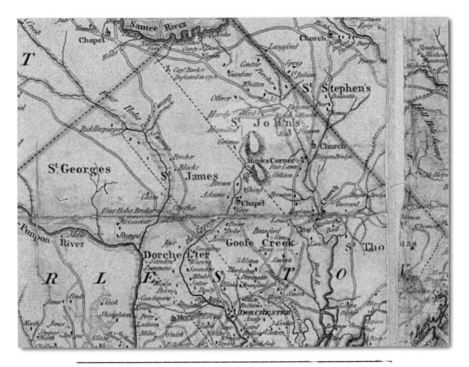

This map of St. Johns Parish was created in the 1770s.
Francis Marion moved to the area in 1751 with his mother.
He helped with his brother Gabriel's farm until he could
purchase his own land. St. Johns is highlighted in yellow above.

Pond Bluff, in upper St. Johns. Francis was close to his brothers, and it is presumed that he still spent a lot of time with them.

Francis did not enjoy socializing outside the family, but he learned that he appreciated the beauty and solitude of the swamps. Hunting, which he always enjoyed, became his chief recreation. He roamed the swamps of the low country from Charleston to Georgetown, either with his family or with friends such as Bob James or Baker Johnson. Sometimes

The terrain where Francis Marion roamed with his friends looked much like this. This photo shows a cypress tree growing in the Wambaw Creek Wilderness, in Francis Marion National Forest.

Francis and his companions would roam for days at a time.

Before Francis Marion became a landowner, however, he was a militiaman. At the beginning of the French and Indian War, fought in America from 1754 to 1763, Gabe and Francis Marion joined the militia at St. Johns. In October 1759, the colonial militia was mobilized at Moncks Corner, north of Charleston, because of the threat of an alliance between the Cherokee, Creek, and French. The battles that followed were known as the Cherokee Wars. They began when the Cherokee, angered by problems on the Virginia frontier, attacked Fort Prince George on the South Carolina border, as well as settlers living in the area. South Carolina governor William Lyttleton knew that there was little time to spare. He was afraid that the French at New Orleans, who had already sent agents into Cherokee villages, would succeed in linking the Creek Indians in Georgia and Alabama with the Cherokee. In the past,

This engraving shows the defeat of General Braddock in the French and Indian War, in Virginia, in 1755. Both the British and the French were fighting over land rights and the rich natural resources in America. Despite what the name of the war implies, both sides had Indian allies.

such problems were often dealt with by negotiating. However, the governor refused to negotiate with the Cherokee and instead sought to intimidate them. He did this by assembling the militia and then taking Cherokee leaders hostage. If these tactics failed, he planned to march on the Cherokee towns and destroy them. When the Indians ignored his first efforts, Lyttleton met the militia at Moncks Corner. He selected the best men from the militia, including Francis Marion, and added to them "gentlemen of fortune, serving as volunteers . . .[and] . . . regulars from the

This is a 1796 portrait of Royal Governor William Henry
Lyttleton by George Romney. Lyttleton was governor of
South Carolina from 1756 to 1760. He would then be
appointed as governor of Jamaica, another British colony.

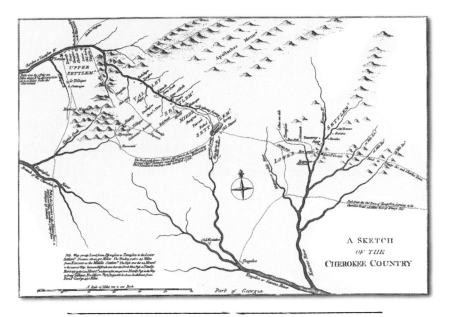

This 1760 map by J. Lodge shows the Cherokee villages in South Carolina. Since the arrival of Europeans in America, the Cherokee and other Indian tribes had steadily been pushed west. Though technically allied with the British since the 1720s, the Cherokee still conducted raids, and colonists still killed Cherokees who "trespassed" on their land. By the late 1750s, all-out war was declared.

Independent companies . . ." assigned to defend the colony. The force of 1,500 men marched slowly northward. After much delay, including an outbreak of smallpox, and no combat, Lyttleton negotiated a treaty with the Cherokee that failed to resolve the conflict. In spring 1760, a second expedition, under Colonel Archibald Montgomery, also failed to make the tribe cooperate or to guarantee the safety of the settlers on the frontier.

In May 1761, Lieutenant Colonel James Grant led 2,500 English regulars, South Carolina militia, and some Chickasaw and Catawba Indians into North

Carolina in pursuit of the Cherokee. On June 10, his advance guard, including friendly Indians and thirty men under Lieutenant Francis Marion, was sent forward searching for an ambush. The enemy was found 8 miles (12.9 km) south of Franklin, North Carolina, at Cowhowee. In the three-hour battle that followed, Marion's small command was all but wiped out. The sacrifice, however, revealed the Cherokee's hidden locations and enabled Grant's regulars to drive them from the area.

Militarily, Grant's campaign was a success. In little more than three months, his command marched hundreds of miles, burned fifteen villages, including large supplies of corn and beans, and forced the Cherokee into the high mountains. The peace that followed lasted for two decades.

Still, the Cherokee won a partial victory. As they retreated farther into the mountains, they avoided open combat, for which they lacked the weapons and ammunition. They limited themselves to fighting from behind trees and rocks, where they were protected. While Grant gave the order to "put every Soul to Death" and destroyed their food with the idea that the Cherokee "must perish in the winter," the Cherokee

---

Opposite: This is a map of North Carolina from 1780. During the battles with the Cherokee, Francis Marion was sent toward North Carolina to scout out ambushes. It was during these missions that Marion gained valuable experience in tactics, including the idea of avoiding open combat and using ambush and surprise to fight a foe with greater numbers.

held to their strategy and survived. In the end, the rugged terrain of the mountains and the continued resistance of the Cherokee forced an end to the conflict.

These expeditions were a learning experience, both positive and negative, for Francis Marion. On the positive side, he saw that, unlike Lyttleton, Grant maintained discipline, ignored the petty quarrels of his subordinates, and made good decisions. Marion came to understand that one of the reasons Grant stayed in control was because Grant, as Marion put it, "never consults anybody," thereby eliminating long debates and the possibility of being overheard. Marion also came to admire the Cherokee for their ability to live off the land, and their decision to fight and run instead of engaging the British in open battle. In addition, he watched with interest, and probably some disapproval, as the militia and friendly Indians disappeared, or deserted, when there was no activity or if they did not agree with an order. On the negative side, he probably had little respect for Lyttleton's abilities and was taken aback at the harshness of Grant's discipline. The lieutenant colonel executed seven men for attempting to desert and destroyed the Cherokee winter food supply with little thought to the lives of the women and children.

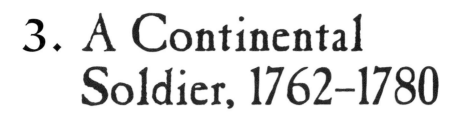

3. A Continental Soldier, 1762–1780

At the age of twenty-nine, with his military service done, Francis Marion returned to St. Johns Parish. He expected to go back to hunting and to finish out an otherwise undistinguished career working the land. He maintained his relationship with his brothers Job and Gabe. When Gabe died in 1767, Francis and Job, probably with the permission of Isaac, Benjamin, and Esther, sold their parents' remaining property in Georgetown. At the same time, Francis seemed to take on some of Gabe's former responsibilities. He served as a tax inquirer and collector and regularly took part in militia drills. Although he was not a good speaker, he was interested in local politics and was popular with the "middling sort," or middle class, because he was more like them. Although his exact political views are not known, and he may not have favored independence from England in the early 1770s, it seems likely that he did. Available information shows that he and his family seem to have sided with those in the colony who felt that the colonists in the Assembly, not the royal governor, should control South Carolina.

Things were starting to heat up in the colonies at this time. Several acts, passed by the British parliament and King George III to raise money after the French and Indian War, were causing quite a stir. The British had tried to enforce taxes already in place, called the Navigation Acts, but the colonists grumbled so much that the British did not make a lot of money. Instead they imposed the Stamp Act on the colonies in 1765, and, later, in 1773, the Tea Act. The colonists

This cartoon was published in a London newspaper on the day the king repealed the Stamp Act. The cartoon made fun of George Grenville, here called George Stamper, and his supporters for this and other unpopular taxes. Grenville carries a small coffin holding his "child," the Stamp Act. The two banners being carried by his supporters represent the parliamentary votes against the act. Also there is box waiting to be shipped to America. It contains a statue of William Pitt, the man who caused the repeal of the tax on printed material.

This Currier lithograph shows the Boston Tea Party of December 16, 1773. The men in the boat were patriots dressed as Mohawk Indians. In protest against a tax on tea, they threw the contents of 342 chests of tea into Boston Harbor, while the colonists cheered them on. The British punished the colonists with the Coercive, or Intolerable, Acts.

were very upset. They felt Parliament had no right to tax them unless they had a voice in the government. In 1773, the Boston Tea Party occurred. Patriots dumped 342 chests of British tea into Boston Harbor. The British punished the colonies with the Coercive Acts, otherwise known as the Intolerable Acts.

As one might imagine, things were quite tense in the colonies by 1774. The South Carolina Assembly, the colony's traditional legislative body, was so divided about what action to take that a special committee had to be formed. In December 1774, Francis Marion and his brother Job were elected to sit in a special assembly called the

General Provincial Congress. This body, which met twice between January 11 and June 18, was to act in place of the South Carolina Assembly. The election was a mark of the community's growing respect and confidence in Francis Marion. The young planter met the minimum requirements for election in that he owned 500 acres of land, possessed at least ten slaves, and owned property worth twenty shillings. He was the least important landholder of the six elected from his parish, however. The General Provincial Congress was to manage the colony's affairs until the crisis over taxation and control by England could be resolved. The Congress also had to coordinate the activities of South Carolina with other colonies that were having problems with the mother country, as England was called.

In June 1775, the Provincial Congress took emergency measures. Congress was nervous because fighting had broken out around Boston, Massachusetts. It ordered the raising of troops, the printing of money, and the removal of executive and legislative power from the hands of the governor and the assembly. The provincial troops, soon to be called Continental soldiers, were twelve-month soldiers who were intended to replace the poorly trained, ill-equipped, and unreliable colonial militia units. They were to be divided into three regiments—two infantry and one cavalry—and were expected to be a disciplined and well-trained force around which the militia could be organized. This project and others were to be financed

This is an undated engraving titled *The Battle of Lexington*. On April 19, 1775, the battles of Lexington and Concord would signal the official beginning of the American Revolution, which would lead to America's independence from Great Britain.

through the printing of paper money. Meanwhile, a council of safety was formed to assume the executive control of South Carolina, and a general committee took on the legislative duties. Each was to serve until the traditional British government could be replaced by a written constitution.

Marion's interest lay with the creation of the new regiments. The delegates to the congress thought enough of his abilities and experience in the Cherokee Wars to make him a leader. Former lieutenant Marion was promoted to captain, third in seniority among the twenty other men chosen, and was placed with the Second Regiment under the command of Colonel William Moultrie. Captain Marion was shortly thereafter sent

This 1782 portrait of Major General William Moultrie was done by Charles Willson Peale. Until 1760, Moultrie was a member of South Carolina's Provincial Assembly. After playing a large role in putting down a Cherokee uprising, he became a leader in his colony's military affairs. Then, early in the Revolution, he was appointed as commander of the Continental army's Second Regiment. The British captured him in 1780, and he remained their prisoner until 1782.

"towards Georgetown, Black River, and Great Pedee" to recruit men for his company. He borrowed expense money from friends in Charleston, and despite the interference of British sympathizers, or Tories, on the Pedee River, he brought back sixty men and began their training.

The commander of the Second Regiment, Colonel William Moultrie, had also been Marion's superior in the Cherokee Wars from 1760 to 1761. Moultrie recognized his junior officer's ability and rewarded him with repeated assignments. In September, Marion's company was one of three assigned to capture Fort Johnson, the only British fort in Charleston Harbor. From November through December, he was instructed to move the "cannon, Gunpowder, Stores & Public Records" of the city of Charleston to Dorchester, 30 miles (48.3 km) north of the city, to prevent them from falling into British hands in the event of an attack. In December, Marion was back in Charleston. He and a part of the Second Regiment with select militia units were assigned to repair Fort Johnson and to construct defensive works at Mount Pleasant. Finally, in February 1776, they were instructed to build a fort at the harbor mouth on the end of Sullivan's Island.

This fort, first known as Fort Sullivan and later as Fort Moultrie, was only half complete on June 28, when a British fleet attacked it. Gunpowder was lacking and Marion, a major since February and in charge of half of

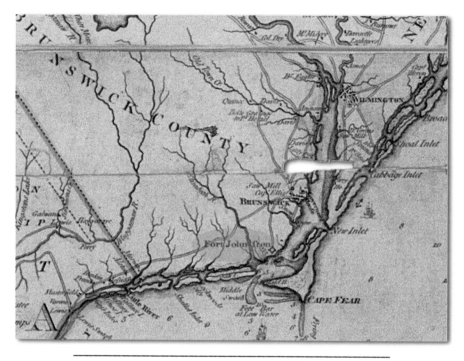

This map from the 1770s shows Fort Johnson highlighted in blue. In 1775, Francis Marion was assigned to capture the fort from the British. He was then assigned to repair and strengthen the fort in case the British tried to regain it.

the fort's thirty-one cannons, was instructed to sight and fire each of his pieces personally to conserve the precious explosive. When the reserve was exhausted, it was Marion who obtained enough gunpowder from a nearby ship to continue firing "until a supply . . . was received from the city." Shortly thereafter, the fleet withdrew. American forces had won a major victory, their last in the South for nearly five years.

From 1776 to 1779, there was little open warfare in the southeast. Marion was promoted first to lieutenant colonel and then to commander of the Second Regiment. To alleviate growing boredom among the Continentals, Colonel Marion required "close training" for officers and men alike. It was soon said that "for cleanliness of person, neatness of dress, and gentlemanly manners, clarity and exactness in performing their evolution [of drill], they soon became the admiration and praise of citizens and soldiers." Lieutentant Colonel Peter Horry would later credit Marion with being the "architect of the Second Regiment."

The Second Regiment's colonel was a strict disciplinarian, a way of life he probably learned from those under whom he had served. He would not tolerate soldiers or officers out of uniform, with beards or long hair, drunk, stealing, missing from duty, or firing off weapons. Yet possibly because of his experience under the ruthless Grant, his demands were tempered by reason. He refused to agree to the execution of disobedient soldiers and limited flogging and other harsh punishments. Humiliation was his discipline of choice. A man out of uniform, for instance, would be publicly reprimanded and sent to get dressed, and a soldier with a beard would be shaved at drill. On one occasion a young lieutenant overstayed a leave that he had obtained under false pretenses. When the young man returned, Marion, in front of his officers, ignored the offender and then remarked coldly: "Lieutenant, is that you? Well, never mind it—there is no harm done—I never missed you." A man deserting would be treated more harshly, receiving a flogging when caught. Even worse to Marion was a soldier "doing his Occasions in and around the fort," or in other words, going to the bathroom in inappropriate places. This lack of cleanliness "must bring Disorders," or sickness, "on every individual if not prevented." Being caught in such an act meant an automatic court-martial, and in the Second Regiment court-martials were frequent. Still, as the lieutenant whom Marion humbled was quick to point out, "the stern, keen-eyed" Marion might be "an ugly, cross, knock-kneed, hook-nosed son of a b—," but he commanded respect.

In December 1778, the arrival of a British force at Savannah brought training to an end. This army, under the command of General Augustine Prevost, quickly captured Savannah and its small garrison and then evaded South Carolina relief forces under Benjamin Lincoln and William Moultrie. In early May, Prevost slipped past Lincoln and Moultrie and came within hours of taking Charleston. The city, defended by only a few hundred men under Marion, was saved because Prevost failed to attack before Lincoln's small army arrived. The British, now outnumbered, slowly withdrew back to Beaufort and Savannah.

Earlier in 1778, the French had become allies with the rebelling American colonies and had sent troops and supplies to aid in the fight against the British. In September 1779, France sent troops and ships under

This is an undated portrait of Augustine Prevost based
on a drawing in the possession of Theodore Prevost. A
soldier said of Prevost's attack on Savannah, "The invasion of
General Prevost was creditable neither to the valor nor the honor
of British soldiers. . . . Private houses were robbed of their plate;
persons of their jewels . . . and three thousand slaves were
carried off and sold . . ." Even in retreat from Charleston,
Prevost managed to carry off hundreds of the colonists' slaves.

Major General Benjamin Lincoln (1733-1810) had experience in dealing with the militia and came highly recommended by George Washington for command of the southern front. He was liked and respected by all who knew him and was expected to reorganize the southern militia while avoiding a major battle. Unfortunately, he was unable to either maneuver troops effectively or to manage the militia he was sent to organize. In addition, he presented a poor example of a commanding officer. According to one authority, he was "fat, dumpy, and lame" and suffered from narcolepsy. This meant that he could fall sound asleep while dictating a dispatch, having a conversation, or managing a battle.

Count D'Estaing to help recapture Savannah. Due to the terms of the treaty, both Lincoln and Moultrie were placed under D'Estaing's command and were summoned to assist him in taking the city. The Count was neither a good soldier nor a good admiral. He first delayed an assault, then surrounded the city as if preparing for a long siege. Finally, he attacked on the morning of October 9. While D'Estaing had wasted all of this time, Prevost had made his fortifications almost impregnable, and the allies suffered heavily.

Colonel Marion was largely a spectator in the campaign. Moultrie had left his junior officer in charge of Charleston's defenses and the army's supplies. Marion soon realized that he lacked the soldiers to defend the city and did not have enough resources or trained personnel to supply an army. When he and his regiment were brought forward for the October assault, he, like others, could not understand why D'Estaing wanted to attack at this late date. Normally a man of few words, the colonel was heard to exclaim: "My God! Who ever heard of anything like this before? First allow an enemy to entrench, and then fight him!" The loss of one of every five men in the assaulting columns only confirmed his worst suspicions, and he considered Lincoln's failure to abandon the siege even more foolish.

In early January 1780, Lincoln learned that Lord Henry Clinton, British commander in chief in America, was sailing southward from New York with a large force.

Sir Henry Clinton replaced William Howe as commander of the British forces in America in 1778, and he met with some early successes. Clinton became known for his intelligent military planning and poor execution of plans. His papers, including many spy letters, intelligence reports, and military maps, are housed at the William L. Clements Library, at the University of Michigan at Ann Arbor.

Lincoln, guessing Clinton's destination, immediately left Savannah and headed for Charleston to prepare for a siege. Colonel Marion, who was left in charge of the army, was to oversee their withdrawal and then to "march immediately for this town." When the soldiers arrived, Lincoln put them to work strengthening the fortifications, hoping to copy Prevost's defense of Savannah, Georgia.

Clinton, a competent professional soldier, took the opportunity that was given him. He arrived south of the city on February 11, with 10,000 men. He methodically surrounded Charleston by April 14, and he forced its surrender on May 12. Thirty-three hundred men, including 2,500 Continental soldiers, surrendered. The troops were not to be released until exchanged for British prisoners. The militia and citizenry were paroled and were sent to their homes with the understanding that they would not be disturbed if they avoided further rebellion. At the same time, British cavalry and infantry swept the countryside, defeated all opponents, and rallied Tory militiamen. By June 4, most men, wrote Lord Henry Clinton, were "either our prisoners or in arms with us."

Through all of this, Marion's departure from Charleston was hardly noticed. The commander of the Second Regiment had been injured, not in combat, but in a fall at a friend's house. He had leaped from the second story of the house to Tradd Street below to

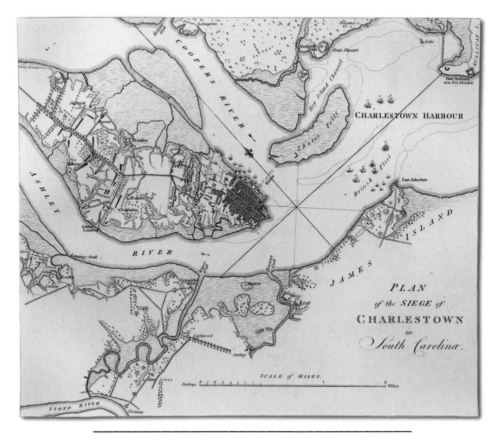

This is a 1787 map showing the plan of the siege of Charleston in South Carolina. This battle would end with the Americans suffering their worst defeat of the war.

avoid a drinking party that was in progress. This mistake severely shattered one of his already weak ankles. Confined to his bed, he was obviously unfit for further command. On April 21, 1780, the colonel and other unnecessary personnel were evacuated from the city to conserve the limited food supply there.

4. The Revolution Renewed, 1780

Benjamin Lincoln's defeat at Charleston was the worst suffered by a patriot army during the American Revolution. It was just the beginning, too. After the victory at Charleston, the British followed up by seizing nine key positions in the Carolinas. They began by taking Augusta on the Savannah River. Then, they captured and built forts at Ninety-Six, Camden, Cheraw, and Georgetown, and they created lesser forts at Hanging Rock, Charlotte, and Rocky Mount. Finally, an army of occupation was established at Camden under Lord Charles Cornwallis to guard the main approach to Charleston. Sir Henry Clinton returned to New York with nearly half of his men on June 5, 1780. To the British, everything appeared to be under control.

Developing events, however, quickly destroyed this sense of security. Key among these events was a proclamation issued by Clinton on June 3, that required all parolees, including those taken at Charleston, to fight for the king upon demand. Because

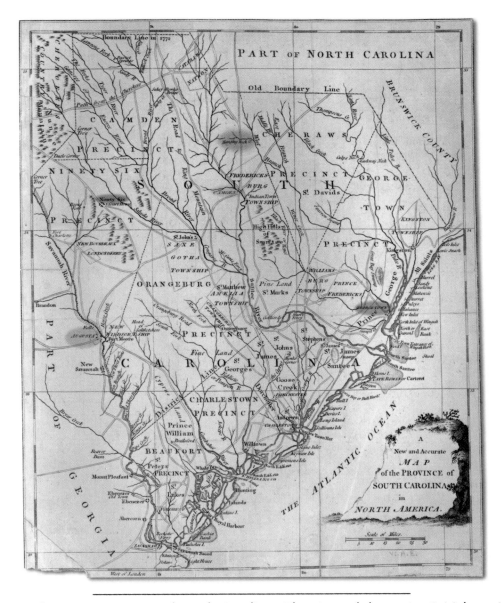

This is a 1780 map of South Carolina. The sites of the major British victories in South Carolina are highlighted above. Augusta is colored orange, Charlotte is yellow, Ninety-Six is highlighted in blue, Camden in green, Georgetown in purple, and Hanging Creek and Rocky Mount are pink. The British had control over Georgia and South Carolina by 1780, and were hopeful that the rest of the South would fall as well. The colonists had not given up the fight, though, and soon the British were not feeling quite so confident.

this went against the surrender terms of May 12, 1780, many parolees were angry. In addition, people who had avoided the struggle in and around Charleston felt that they had been deceived and now considered joining the patriot cause at the first opportunity. Cornwallis added to the unrest by allowing his commissary to purchase food from Tories, or loyalists, in order to feed his soldiers but to take it, without pay, from former patriots. At the same time, Lord George Germain, King George III's minister of war in London, ordered his generals to inflict "fire and sword" upon people who continued to resist or to aid those who fought against the king.

The easy capture of Georgia and South Carolina made Germain, Clinton, and Cornwallis hopeful that North Carolina, Virginia, and the middle colonies—Maryland, Pennsylvania, New Jersey, and New York—could be taken also. Beginning in Georgia, Tory regiments would be raised to guard the line of advance. When Cornwallis united with Clinton, both would then turn on George Washington, destroy his army, conquer New England, and end the war.

Yet scarcely were British fortifications in place when the raising of Tory regiments led to renewed warfare in upper South Carolina. On June 20, a large Tory force was beaten by patriot militia at Ramour's Mill, north of Charlotte. Twenty-three days later, other Tory units were defeated at Cedar Springs, near Spartanburg, and also at

Williamston's Plantation, in York County. Then, on August 5, 1780, Thomas Sumter defeated British infantry and cavalry at Hanging Rock, and Isaac Shelby destroyed another British force at Musgrove Mill near Ninety-Six. This was not the only damage to the British cause. According to British major James Wemyess, "the whole country between [the] Pedee and [the] Santee [Rivers] has ever since been in an absolute state of rebellion, every friend of Government has been carried off, and his plantation destroyed. This unfortunate business, if it should have no worse consequences, will shake the confidence of our friends in this province . . ."

Charles Cornwallis, unprepared for the loss of

This is an undated engraving of British general Charles Cornwallis.

Lieutenant General Charles Cornwallis, First Marquis of Cornwallis, lived from 1738 to 1805. He was an admirable soldier and a fine administrator. He was brave, performed well in battle, and earned the respect of his soldiers. He also enjoyed the support of England's secretary of war, Lord Germain, who appreciated the victory at Camden and wanted more such triumphs for the British. In compliance with private instructions from London, Cornwallis, who had little understanding of guerilla warfare, marched into North Carolina and Virginia before South Carolina was under control. In doing so, he helped to undermine the campaign in the south.

nearly 1,000 men in less than two months, was to experience two additional trials. The first, and the less difficult for him to deal with, was the arrival of a new American army. In April 1780, soldiers from George Washington's army had been sent to South Carolina under the command of the experienced Baron Jean DeKalb. His instructions were to help Charleston or, if the city fell, keep the revolution alive. It was understood that DeKalb was allowed to fight, but only if he thought he could win. In late July, the technical commander of all military forces, the Second Continental Congress, had placed General Horatio Gates in command of DeKalb's men. This force amounted to nearly three thousand militiamen and regulars.

This is an engraved portrait of American general Horatio Gates. Gates lived from 1728 to 1806.

General Horatio Gates, upon assuming his command, ignored the advice of DeKalb and his officers and marched directly toward Camden without knowing that Cornwallis and much of his army were there. On August 21, the two forces met. Gates's militia quickly ran, after brief resistance, and it left the regulars to be destroyed by the British force, which had better training, equipment, and supplies. Horatio Gates panicked and deserted the battlefield shortly after his militia. Many American soldiers, wrote one observer, were "chagrined and mortified at not overtaking their commanding general in so long a retreat"—60 miles (96.5 km). Two days later, Thomas Sumter, who had not arrived in time to assist Gates, was defeated badly, also. This left the British commander Cornwallis undisputedly in control of the colony.

Cornwallis's second trial was Francis Marion, who was, in the meanwhile, just making his appearance. Until now the British general had known nothing of his soon-to-be opponent. After all, according to William Moultrie, Marion had left Charleston "so lame that he was obliged to sulk about from house to house among his friends, and sometimes hid in bushes until he grew better." Marion needed to avoid capture until he was well. Once he had sufficiently healed, "he then crept out by degrees and began to collect a few friends; and when he got ten or twelve together he ventured out."

In July, Francis Marion, with less than two dozen men and boys, both white and black, had joined DeKalb in North Carolina. They were, in the words of DeKalb's second in command, "wretchedly, [even] . . . miserably equipped; their appearance was in fact so

Following Spread: This hand-colored engraving by an unknown artist shows the death of Baron DeKalb at the Battle of Camden, where the colonial army was so thoroughly defeated by General Cornwallis.

burlesque, that it was with much difficulty the dive-sion [derision] of the regular soldiery was restrained by the officers." DeKalb, who was in desperate need of information, sent Marion's force to scout the upper Pedee River for signs of Cornwallis's army. When the men returned, Gates, who was by now in command, dispatched Marion on August 15, to the Black River and Lynches Creek area to "watch the enemy and [to] furnish intelligence." Marion was instructed also to take command of the Williamsburg militia, destroy all boats on the Santee River to hamper Cornwallis's sup-ply system, and then retreat.

Two days later, Marion and the core of what was to become his brigade met for the first time at Witherspoon's Ferry on Lynches Creek. He was described for history by William James, a fifteen-year-old recruit: "He was rather below the middle stature of men, lean and swarthy. His body was well set, but his knees and ankles were badly formed; and he still limped upon one leg. He had a countenance remark-ably steady; his nose was aquiline, his chin projecting; his forehead was large and high, and his eyes black and piercing. He was now forty-eight years of age." Even though the militia were pleased with their new commander, Colonel Marion was disap-pointed momentarily. He considered the appointment a demotion from the regular army, a "sulking position," and he doubted his ability to command militiamen who resisted discipline and came and went as they wished.

Doubts were quickly put to rest as Marion and his new command achieved small but important victories— August 20, at Great Savannah, September 4, at Blue Savannah, September 28, at Black Mingo, and October 26, at Tearcot Swamp. These successes were achieved by surprise and long marches. Each battle was fought in a way designed to allow the fewest casualties, and all brought in supplies of weapons and equipment, ammunition, food, and horses. In the process, Marion developed a winning style of fighting, which slowly attracted militia recruits and kept them beyond their regular two-month term of service. With these new men, he added to the number of units under his command and expanded the area of his operations. These independent companies, the backbone of his emerging organization, formed little more than a small regiment, but they were soon divided into two commands, one under Hugh Horry and the other under Hugh's brother, Peter Horry.

Marion's rules of war were based upon the successes and failures of men that he had served under, such as Lyttleton, Moultrie, Grant, and Lincoln. They were also based on what he had learned from enemies, like Prevost and the Cherokee, whom he had come to admire. First and foremost was rapid movement and surprise. He always struck in the early morning, when his enemy was least prepared to resist. His victories at

Great Savannah and Blue Savannah required a hard, pre-dawn ride, while Black Mingo and Tearcot Swamp took two full days and nights in the saddle to reach their unsuspecting victims.

Accurate information on the enemy was critical. His commanders supplied their best men mounted on their fastest horses to guard all trails and roads from the Santee to the Pedee Rivers. They were to inform Marion of any enemy movements. More specialized intelligence agents, guides, and spies, like Bob James, Baker Johnson, and Gavin Witherspoon, arrived almost hourly and departed for unknown destinations that they or their commander thought worthy of checking. These and other men reported only to Marion and were expected not to repeat what they had learned, even to their friends. Men such as these neither served as guards nor performed normal military duties, but it was understood that they were to be ready whenever Marion wanted them. In return they had a special relationship with their commander. They laughed or joked with him, often at his own expense, and hunted and fished with him as they had always done. They did his bidding without question, but they did it on their own terms. Baker Johnson, for instance, galloped into camp with important news on one occasion but had not eaten for days. His superiors ordered him to report to Marion immediately, but he refused, saying that he was starving and that the colonel could come to him. Marion quickly did so without complaint.

The colonel, who seldom slept, individually questioned local men and women, slaves, and even prisoners of war in a never-ending search for information. Members of the Williamsburg District soon competed with one another to help him. In each of the battles mentioned, it was special intelligence that gave his command the advantages that they needed. In Great Savannah, he received information from a deserter. At Blue Savannah and Tearcot Swamp, advance patrols warned him. Black Mingo was won thanks to information from prisoners of war. At the same time, Marion denied similar intelligence to the enemy by carefully screening those who could leave or enter the district. "There should be no communication between the inhabitants of your district and Georgetown," was an all-too-familiar order to his border commanders. Only the name of the place, from Georgetown to Charleston to Fort Motte and so on, would change. Those caught giving information to the British were stripped of their property.

Good horses were second in importance only to information. Mobility was important, but speed was even more essential. Marion's brigade was poorly armed, often only with shotguns, quail guns, or homemade swords, and ammunition was scarce, making it necessary for Marion's patrols to call off an action if they were out-

gunned, or if their supply of ammunition was exhausted. To men who were so desperate for ammunition that
they saved the balls they were shot with in order to fire
them back, retreat was not a disgrace. Escape was an
opportunity to fight again, and the horse was the means
to flee. As a result, Marion's men prized their animals
above all else and refused to surrender them, even to
other American units. Francis Marion, for example, carried a sword and pistols, but his sword was rusty, and he
was a poor shot with his pistol. Yet he was extremely
proud of his large, fast horse, named Ball, and took better care of Ball than he took of himself. A friend, Captain
John James, had an equally powerful animal, known as
Thunder, and fourteen-year-old James Gwynne possessed a beautiful brown horse, named Otterskin.
Marion presented Gwynne with the horse after Gwynne
calmly stood before a charge of ten men and shot its rider
from the saddle. In doing so, Gwynne had saved the life
of Peter Horry and had stopped the charge.

The colonel likewise believed in personal planning
and constant movement to avoid being surprised.
Seldom did the command remain at the same campsite
for more than two days. It was even less likely that
Marion would share the planning process with anyone,
including his subordinates, for fear of being accidental-
ly or intentionally betrayed or overheard. The first
thing that anyone heard of a raid was the order to
mount and ride, usually before dawn for a morning

This hand-colored engraving from the 1800s shows Francis Marion on his horse. Strong, fast horses were necessary because of Marion's tactics of lightning attacks. Marion had weak legs, so traveling on horseback was the only way he could be a successful soldier.

raid, or at dusk for a night in the saddle. Yet the men soon learned to look for the telltale sign of movement, the cooking of unusual amounts of food. Second only to Bob James, Marion trusted his long-term body servant and friend, Oscar. When Oscar quietly began roasting potatoes, the brigade's main source of food, observers would count the number, divide by two for Oscar and Marion, and quickly prepare an equal number for themselves. The more potatoes that Oscar cooked, the longer the ride.

Tactics were important also. The colonel knew that "the enemy knew better how to defend forts and entrenched places than we did and that if we attempted it, we should fall into their hands." It was his opinion that only "the open field was our play," but even there he required an advantage, or an edge, and refused to attack an enemy who was waiting for him. Surprise, not the sword or the musket, was his main weapon. At Great Savannah and Blue Savannah, as at other battles, he divided his units. Each operated independently from him, but with specific orders. One would attack the British force from behind, and, then, when the English turned to meet the threat, the other unit would come from the front. At Black Mingo and Tearcot Swamp, the attack came from three fronts: the left and right flanks, and, finally, the center. The system worked best when Marion was well informed and his opponent unprepared. In November 1780, the colonel, then operating with more than two hundred men, became bolder. By this time, Lord Cornwallis was aware of the problem of "Mr. Marion," and sent his best commander, Colonel Banastre Tarleton, with his legion, in pursuit of the Williamsburg men. Tarleton, with information obtained from a local slave, set a trap near Jack's Creek and almost caught his opponent. Marion, however, was warned by a local widow and quickly retreated. Tarleton's legion pursued him through miles of swamp. At Benbow's Ferry, Marion found the battlefield for which he was looking. He halted his men, cut trees to make a barricade, and prepared to fight. Tarleton, whether due to wisdom or the exhaustion of his troops, refused the challenge, and the British colonel supposedly uttered, "Come my boys! Let us go back, and we will find the Gamecock [Sumter], but as for this damned old fox, the Devil himself could not catch him." Thus Francis Marion became known as the Swamp Fox.

The first year of Marion's command ended quietly, but successfully. Recruits were on the increase and the morale of the colony and Francis Marion's district, in particular, was improved, despite increased British and Tory raids. There were also indications that there would be renewed warfare to follow in the up-country. The indicators proved true. In early October, Cornwallis lost more than one thousand men at King's Mountain along the North Carolina border. The following month,

This oil painting of General Sir Banastre Tarleton was done by Joshua Reynolds in 1782.

Lieutenant Colonel Banastre Tarleton (1754-1833) joined the British army in 1775, and he fought so well that he was promoted to colonel and was given command of the British Legion in 1778. Tarleton commanded Cornwallis's cavalry in the Carolina campaign, and he was noted for his rapid movements, hard-hitting attacks, and swift and relentless pursuits. His policy of total war, including burning homes, destroying food supplies, executing potential enemies, and killing soldiers who surrendered, earned him the nickname of Bloody Ban. Patriots soon began to use the words "Tarleton's Quarter" to justify the killing of Tories when they were captured.

Thomas Sumter defeated Tarleton at Blackstocks, near Union. Two months later, on December 2, 1780, Major General Nathanael Greene took charge of what was left of the southern army. He began the reorganization of this unit and the coordination of all forces south of Maryland. As part of this effort, Francis Marion was commissioned a brigadier general of militia with control of all regiments east of the Santee, Wateree, and Catawba Rivers.

5. Winning the Revolution, 1781–1782

The quiet that carried over into the new year of 1781 was deceiving, for much was being accomplished. First Francis Marion's irregulars effectively shut down the Santee River, the easiest supply line between Camden and Charleston. The British had to send their provisions and equipment via Moncks Corner, the Congaree River, and finally Camden. To do this, they had to establish a new line of forts—Granby, Motte, Nelson's Ferry, and Moncks Corner. Of course, soldiers were needed to guard these facilities, and this further drained the British army's supply of men.

At the same time, a storage depot and retreat was established by Marion at Snow Island, or Goddard's Plantation, above Georgetown on the Pedee River. The island, encircled by rivers, creeks, swamps, and streams, was a natural hideaway. However, the advantages were

---

Opposite: This 1780 map shows the new line of forts that the British had to establish when Marion shut down the Santee River. Fort Granby is highlighted with a yellow triangle, Motte is marked with a rectangle, Nelson's Ferry has an oval, and Moncks Corner is indicated by a circle.

PART OF NORTH CAROLINA

Boundary Line in 1772

Old Boundary Line

BRUNSWICK COUNTY

CAMDEN PRECINCT

TY SIX

CHERAWS

SOUTH

FREDERICKS BURG
CAMDEN
Indian Town TOWNSHIP

PRECINCT
St. Davids

GEORGE-TOWN

KINGSTON TOWNSHIP

High Hills of Santee

PRECINCT

Kingston

Ninety Six
Court House

SAXE GOTHA TOWNSHIP

BOURDEAUX
ONDONDERRY

St. John's

WILLIAMS BURG TOWNSHIP

PRINCE FREDERICKS

George

ORANGEBURG

St. Matthew
AMELIA TOWNSHIP

Pine Land
St. Marks

GEORGE TOWN

Prince

Orangeburg Road

ORANGEBURG TOWNSHIP

NEW WINDSOR TOWNSHIP
Fort Moore

Head of Saltketchers

Orangeburg

PRECINCT

CAROLINA

Fine Land
Line

St. James

St. Johns

Georges

Stephens
St. James Santee

St. James Swamp

North Santee

South Santee

Shoal

Goose Creek

CAPE ROMAN or Carteret

Monks Corner

DORCHESTER

CHARLESTOWN

PRECINCT

St. Andrews
CHARLESTOWN
Charles Town Bar

Prince William
Brailsford

BEAUFORT

St. Peters

PRECINCT

Willtown

Stono Inlet
Keywaw Isle
Simmons Isle
North Eddisto

St. HELENA SOUND

Mount Pleasant

St. Lukes

Hunting Islands

Ebenezer
Old Town
Ebenezer

Abercorn

Port Royal Harbour

SAVANNAH

Savannah Sound
Light House

GIA

THE ATLANTIC OCEAN

A
New and Accurate
MAP
of the PROVINCE of
SOUTH CAROLINA
in
NORTH AMERICA.

Scale of Miles.
5 10 15 20 25 30

West of London

This nineteenth-century wood engraving shows
Francis Marion's encampment at Snow Island on the
Pedee River. Having a secure base with sufficient supplies
made it much easier to plan and launch surprise attacks.

increased by a redoubt with cannon and a permanent garrison to guard the Pedee side. The destruction of all bridges and trails leading to the base also helped to keep the soldiers safe. Concealed shelters, storage bins, and a prison called the bull pen were constructed in the wooded section. A number of boats were hidden in the various creeks surrounding the island. All of the other boats between the coast and Nelson's Ferry were destroyed. This base was a huge help to the brigade. Normally they were forced to travel with only one blanket each for shelter. Food was eaten cold because fires could be seen by the enemy, and even hunting and fishing were not allowed. Finally the men had a place to escape bad weather or to relax for several days at a time. The base also permitted the men to bring food from home, cast musket balls, and care for their horses and weapons. For the wounded, it was a long-term recovery camp.

Finally, the arrival of Marion's brigadier commission on January 1, 1781, led to a twofold reorganization of his companies. Colonel Adam McDonald, a talented newcomer to the unit, was placed in charge of the main regiment. This regiment contained five companies of mounted infantry and one special company of proven marksmen. Majors Hugh Horry and John James assisted McDonald. Colonel Peter Horry was given command of the second regiment, which was often called cavalry. This unit, smaller than

McDonald's, contained only four companies of mounted infantry and differed in that its men lacked muskets. Horry's men were expected to obtain weapons or to have saws shaped into swords. A brigade staff that included a second in command, a secretary, and two aides, was created even though Marion still made his decisions privately. He also formalized the system of the mess, or groups of soldiers who ate together, by expanding his own to include not just Oscar but Hugh Horry, Captain James Postel, and Sergeant Davies. He also used the reorganization, on a second level, to remove popular but ineffective leaders from direct command of troops. Some on the "blacklist" were given jobs, but for many there was no official place. They remained loosely attached to Marion's command, retained their rank if they had one, and were used as aides or on individual assignments.

While this was taking place, Marion planned several ambushes and raids. None succeeded, however. A mission against Georgetown on November 15 failed, and in the process his favorite nephew, Gabriel Marion III, was killed. In December, an effort to capture newly established Fort Upton on the Wateree River was cut short when Peter Horry's men got hold of apple brandy. His men told Horry that it was apple water, but they were soon visibly and audibly drunk. When their guide fell off his horse, the expedition had to be called off. Finally, a week later, Marion himself was embarrassingly outmaneuvered by a British major who understood more about guerilla war than did any of his peers.

The British, however, were largely unaware that these were failures. They were very disturbed that Marion was able to disrupt their supply line at will, despite their best efforts to "punish severely" those who assisted him. They were likewise alarmed that the threat or rumor of his appearance was as good as an actual strike. Peter Horry's December failure, for instance, turned out to be a success. His proposed victims heard the drunken revelers approaching them, and, being "exceedingly frightened," all but twenty deserted. Marion, usually very serious, was heard to chuckle when he told Horry that he had done well considering the circumstances, but that he needed "to keep a careful eye on the Apple water next time."

Cornwallis, preparing his force for the northern invasion, found such events less than humorous. He could not permit his supply line to Charleston to be cut.

Charles Cornwallis lived from 1738 to 1805. Probably the most capable British general in the war, he went on to become the governor-general of India and then viceroy of Ireland.

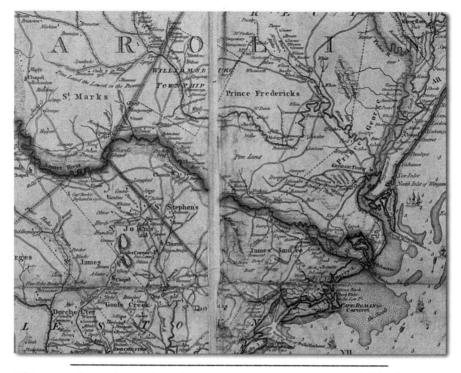

This map from the 1700s shows Francis Marion's main field of operations in South Carolina. They spanned from the Pedee River, highlighted in orange, to the Santee River, highlighted in blue. His knowledge of the wilderness in this area allowed him to launch surprise attacks and then retreat into the wilderness before the British could regroup.

"Colonel Marion had so wrought on the minds of the people . . . that there was scarcely an inhabitant between the Santee and the Pedee that was not in arms against us." To stop this, British and Tory soldiers hung suspected patriots and burned houses and crops. Their actions, far from hurting the Swamp Fox, only brought in more recruits to his cause and as much food as their families could spare. If this was not enough, Marion, like Cornwallis, took supplies from friends but left receipts. From his enemies he took food, without receipts, and he captured the men of the house whenever possible. Unlike Cornwallis, however, he forbade his men to destroy homes and crops, because it left women and children, even if they were Tories, to suffer unnecessarily. Still he was never able to stop all retaliation. Tory prisoners were beaten badly often or even were hung. The man suspected of betraying young Gabriel was executed in camp while being held for questioning. Lord Francis Rawdon, Cornwallis's subordinate and successor, knew that the British policy of "fire and sword" was failing and that he needed to "drive Marion out of that Country, but I cannot yet say what steps I shall take to effect it."

The transfer of what remained of Horatio

Lieutenant Colonel Francis, Lord Rawdon (1754–1826), like Tarleton, joined the British army in 1775 and rose through merit by the age of twenty-six to succeed Lord Cornwallis as commander of South Carolina. He defeated Nathanael Greene at Hobkirk's Hill, outside Camden, while Marion and Lee were burning Fort Motte, and saved Ninety-Six from capture by Greene two months later. He was ranked as one of the most able British officers to fight in the American Revolution.

This is a portrait of Lord Francis Rawdon. On May 24, 1781, Rawdon wrote a letter to Cornwallis. Basically, he said that after all the attacks by Marion, Lee, and Sumter, he was doubtful of keeping control of the South: "Balfour . . . stated, that the revolt was universal, and that . . . the old works of Charles town . . . was inadequate to oppose any force of the consequence; and that the defection of the town's people shewed itself in a thousand instance. I agreed with him in the conclusion to be drawn . . .that any misfortune happening to my corps might entail the loss of the province."

Gates's army to Nathanael Greene made Marion's men even more effective. Greene was willing to loan the Swamp Fox regular cavalry and infantry for short periods of time in order that the general might attack major targets. On January 23, for instance, Colonel Henry "Light Horse Harry" Lee's legion of 250 men joined Marion for an assault upon Georgetown. Their combined troops caught the British off guard and captured numerous officers and men, but failed to secure the fort. Still, coming at the same time as a British defeat at Cowpens on January 17, 1781, the Georgetown assault further disturbed Lord Rawdon at Camden. In early March, Rawdon sent a large British force under Colonel John Watson down the Santee, with a smaller one in support.

Marion met Watson near Murray's Ferry on the north side of the Santee and lured him, as he had Tarleton months earlier, into the swamps. The men of Marion's brigade blocked the trails and destroyed the bridges. It was McDonald's company of sharpshooters that did the most devastating work, however. They picked off Watson's sentries, and, especially his officers. Watson was soon trapped in the quagmires, or bogs, between the Santee and Black Rivers. It took the invader a little more than a week to conclude that he had lost control of the situation. To save his men, he needed to abandon his equipment, including four cannon, and withdraw to Georgetown. As Watson withdrew, news

Lieutenant Colonel Henry Lee was born in Virginia and lived from 1756 to 1818. Lee was educated at Princeton, and, except for the war, might have become a lawyer or a planter. In 1776, he raised three companies of cavalry, joined George Washington's army, and distinguished himself by capturing a British garrison at Paulus Hook in 1779.

He was promoted to lieutenant colonel the following year and was given three additional companies of infantry that became known collectively as Lee's Legion. At Nathanael Greene's request, he was assigned to the southern department and served well in a number of battles. He was called Light Horse Harry because his legion was light cavalry, meaning lightly armed horsemen, and he was known for his lightning strikes against the British.

This is a nineteenth-century engraving of Henry Lee, who was very helpful to Francis Marion during the American Revolution. Lee would serve as governor of Virginia from 1792 to 1795.

This engraving shows the site of Fort Watson. In 1781, Lee and his legion joined Francis Marion and his brigade in a siege of Fort Watson, which was built on an Indian mound. A tall log tower was erected with a platform on top shielding riflemen who overlooked the fort. The British surrendered. Today Fort Watson Memorial is on the banks of Lake Francis Marion on the Congaree River.

arrived from Colonel Hugh Ervin, Marion's second in command. Watson's backup force had captured and burned the brigade's secret base at Snow Island.

The loss of the secure camp, weapons, and ammunition was a major setback for Marion and his men. Although there were more soldiers than ever before, the unit was without supplies, and ammunition was down to less than two rounds per man. In addition, Watson, having recovered at Georgetown, was again threatening the district. Marion was very discouraged.

The growth of forts around his district meant that the British could undercut his intelligence network and strike at him at any time, as Watson's backup force had at Snow Island. The continued existence of these forts also revealed to his enemy that Marion lacked the personnel and knowledge to threaten or take the strongholds. It was only a matter of time until his enemies combined against him as Marion and Lee had done against Watson. On April 9, Marion called a staff meeting to discuss abandoning the locality. Before a decision could be reached, Baker Johnson returned with the news that Lee's legion was on the march to reinforce Marion once again. Other messages indicated that Cornwallis's army had advanced into North Carolina, gained a costly victory at Guilford Courthouse on March 15, 1781, and that Greene was returning to South Carolina with the intention of taking Camden. Greene requested that all militia units report for duty to support his effort.

The brigade quickly recovered its spirit. Henry Lee's men arrived on April 14, and departed the next morning with Francis Marion and his command to attack Fort Watson on the Congaree River. Ammunition, of course, was almost nonexistent, but with regular troops the Swamp Fox stood a chance against the fortified positions that were increasingly limiting his movements.

The daring enterprise began on April 16, and it took eight days to complete. Because the fort was on a

This is a plan of the Battle of Guilford (spelled Guildford on the map), which occurred on March 15, 1781. Though Cornwallis defeated Greene's army, it was at a huge cost. Some historians say this defeat was what sent Cornwallis to Yorktown and led to his eventual surrender to the Continental army.

hill and protected by three lines of trenches, neither Marion nor Lee was willing to throw away lives on a direct assault. Instead they cut the water supply from the nearby lake and waited for the soldiers inside to surrender. The British, however, hung on and completed a well on April 18. As this was happening, smallpox broke out in the American camp. Marion and Lee's troops began to desert to escape the disease. At this point, one of Marion's colonels, Hezekiah Maham, rescued the seige. He built a crude tower that overlooked the fort and enabled the attackers to shoot down upon the garrison. It was complete and in place by April 23. Within hours the fort gave up. The first of the fortifications that supported Lord Rawdon at Camden were gone.

Two weeks later, on May 6, the joint command moved against yet another of Camden's subforts, Fort Motte. This fort, a stronger and better one than Fort Watson, served as the main storage depot for both Camden and Ninety-Six. The center of the stronghold was a large, two-story house belonging to Mrs. Rebecca Motte. The residence, which sat on top of a hill, was confiscated by the British in 1780, and it was surrounded by a stockade, a parapet, and a deep ditch. If Motte and Granby on the Congaree River and Nelson's Ferry on the Santee River could be taken, Lord Rawdon would be forced to abandon Camden and withdraw toward Charleston. Still Motte was too close to Camden to allow even an eight-day siege. Fort Motte had to be taken quickly, and fire was the

This is a portrait of Rebecca Motte by J. W. Orr. She was the daughter of Robert Brewton, an English gentleman who settled in Charleston, South Carolina. In 1758, Rebecca married Jacob Motte, and Buckhead became her summer residence. In 1780, Lord Rawdon made Mrs. Motte's home a British post and had it fortified. It became known as Fort Motte.

This undated, hand-colored woodcut shows
Rebecca Motte and Marion's men preparing to burn
Fort Motte. The figure representing Mrs. Motte in this
picture is based on a portrait owned by her descendants.

only alternative. When this was suggested to Mrs. Motte,
who lived nearby, she agreed, saying, "If it was a palace it
should go." She also contributed the bow and arrows necessary to set the roof on fire. As at Fort Watson, the garrison quickly put up a white flag. On the same day,
Rawdon abandoned the forts at Camden and Nelson's
Ferry and retreated to Moncks Corner. Thomas Sumter
then took Orangeburg, and Lee forced the surrender of
Fort Granby.

When he was no longer encircled, Marion was able to establish a new base at Webdo, or Peyre's Plantation, on the Santee River. Like Snow Island, streams, swamps, and the river made it difficult to access Webdo, and the usual hidden huts and storage bins were constructed. The Swamp Fox had learned another lesson from previous attacks. He would never again leave all of his supplies in one lair. Provisions and equipment were hidden all over the district.

With a new, secure base of operation, Marion set out on May 22, against the last stronghold in his region—Georgetown. All along the way, militia joined the brigade, until they numbered more than five hundred. It was more like a victory parade than an attack. This manpower was more than enough to force the surrender of the city on June 5. Patriot forces then could use Georgetown to import supplies, and Marion, remembering his earlier failure to capture the town, felt good. Only Charleston, the capital and largest city of the colony, remained in British hands.

It was fortunate that Georgetown was a triumph, for the remainder of 1781 and 1782 would bring more crises than opportunities to Francis Marion. A feud developed between Peter Horry and Hezekiah Maham, involving recruiting, horses, and jurisdiction. Although Marion eventually decided in favor of Maham, both subcommanders were angry with each other and with their mutual friend's supposed lack of

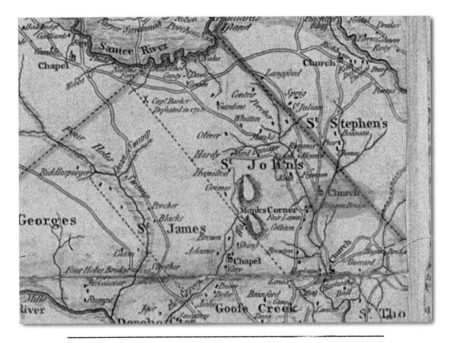

This 1770s map shows Biggins Church, the site of a raid by Francis Marion, Henry Lee, and Thomas Sumter. Sumter directed the assault, and, against the advice of Marion and Lee, launched the attack without proper planning or supplies. The church is highlighted in orange above.

support. Cooperation between the two men became nonexistent.

A raid on Biggin Church, on July 17, also forced the Swamp Fox to attack by frontal assault, a move he had so far refused to undertake. The number of unnecessary casualties suffered was predictable, and it showed exactly why he had refused to undertake such battles in the past. The attack was launched at the command of Thomas Sumter, the ranking officer. Marion, Lee, Horry, and Maham were directed to surround British

This portrait of Thomas Sumter was done by Rembrandt Peale in 1796.

Brigadier General Thomas Sumter (1734-1832) was born on the Virginia frontier but later moved to the Eutaw Springs area in South Carolina. He was very popular with his adopted countrymen and was a natural leader. With the surrender of Charleston in 1780, Sumter turned to guerilla warfare and was soon known as the Blue Hen's Chicken and the Gamecock for his fighting ability. Although he could fight, he was careless in battle, understood little about tactics or strategy, and would not hesitate to risk his men in costly frontal assaults. "Enchanted with the splendor of victory," wrote Henry Lee, "he would wade in torrents of blood to attain it."

units south of Biggin Church. Although a victory was won, Sumter's poor planning and refusal to wait for artillery led to heavy losses for Marion and Lee. Neither commander would serve again under Sumter.

Nathanael Greene's need for an effective militia organization to fight alongside him also contributed to the problems. When Sumter withdrew from military service after the battle at Biggin, Francis Marion became the militia coordinator for much of the state. As such, he commanded not only his own brigade, but also the troops from the middle of the state. His area of responsibility stretched from the Cape Fear River to the city of Savannah.

Nathanael Greene (1742–1786) was a Rhode Island blacksmith who overcame a poor education, his Quaker background, and the opposition of the Second Continental Congress to became one of George Washington's closest military advisers and favorite generals. Between 1778 and 1780, Greene served as Washington's quartermaster general. He reorganized supply, transportation, and equipment for the army. On the basis of this exceptional accomplishment, the "fighting Quaker" was given the command of the southern armies, following Horatio Gates's August 1780 failure at Camden. He fought three important battles—Guilford Courthouse, Hobkirk Hill, and Eutaw Springs. Even though he lost each one, he crippled the two British field armies and kept his own fit and ready to fight.

Charles Willson Peale painted this portrait of
Nathanael Greene in 1733. Greene, born in Rhode Island,
lived from 1742 to 1786. Greene had a saying that summed
up the spirit of the colonists fighting for independence against
all odds. He said, "We fight, get beat, rise, and fight again!"

As senior militia general, Francis Marion found that the independence of the Swamp Fox had to give way to military order. He appointed secretaries to write his dispatches and aides to carry them to scattered commands. The raider became the arbitrator and peacemaker. He even found himself abandoning the swamps for settled, well-known headquarters like Fair Lawn Plantation. Yet the temptation to revert to character was always there. In late August 1781, for instance, Tory gatherings on the Edisto River forced him to take action. After sending part of his command to raid Moncks Corner, he led nearly two hundred men over

This 1844 wood engraving by an unknown artist shows Francis Marion and his brigade defeating Major Frazier at Parkers Ferry. The battle occurred on August 29, 1781, and was a victory for Marion.

This is an undated engraving of the Battle of Eutaw Springs by F. C. Yohn. The battle took place on September 8, 1781. General Alexander Stewart, Rawdon's replacement as commander of the British forces in South Carolina, won the battle, but his force was too damaged for further combat.

100 miles (161 km) through the swamps to Parkers ferry, near Jacksonboro. On August 29, he surprised and routed nearly four hundred enemy troops near the Ferry. Then, as silently as he had come, he moved to his base at Peyre's Plantation on the Santee. There he received orders on September 4, from Greene, to join the main army above Eutaw Springs.

Four days later, General Francis Marion and three militia brigades led Greene's advance at the Battle of Eutaw Springs. His men, who were probably expected to flee as the militia under Horatio Gates had at Camden, held firm. They fired volley after volley, seventeen in all, charged the British and were countercharged by them, and only retreated when their ammunition was gone. Marion's brigade alone lost more than one hundred men during the fight, but Greene recognized the sacrifice. In a letter to a friend, he wrote, "Such conduct would have graced the soldiers of the King of Prussia." Greene's Continentals performed equally well and succeeded in driving a part of the British army from the field. A portion, however, was not enough, and one last attack by the British forced back Greene's men. Still they had done what they had come to do. The militia under Marion had held firm, and Camden was avenged.

The last year of the war was anticlimactic. Neither side possessed the manpower or the ammunition to fight a major battle, and both knew that peace was at that moment being decided in Paris, France. General Marion was responsible for obtaining intelligence from the Charleston area and for preventing the British from raiding beyond the confines of the city. He was authorized also to actively recruit former Tories with the promise that six months' service or more would bring a pardon. This latter assignment was not a popular one, particularly among the men and families of his brigade who had seen their towns pillaged and their homes burned by these same Tories. Despite this, Marion, along with other prominent patriot leaders,

FRIDERICUS II. REX PRUSSIÆ.

This is a portrait of Frederick II, king of Prussia. Also known as Frederick the Great, he lived from 1712 to 1786. He was known as a military genius and was very strict in the training of his soldiers. Greene's quote about the Continentals' performance during the Eutaw Springs battle was a great compliment, meaning that even the superbly trained soldiers of the king of Prussia could not have performed better.

knew that the state would need such men later and carried out the task as best he could.

His brigade increased in numbers during 1782, but it declined in efficiency. Two heavily Tory regiments were added, but, as they were introduced, many of his best men refused to serve. Some hated the new recruits, and others felt that their services were needed more at home. Most just slipped away, as they had always done when the need was greater elsewhere, but some openly challenged their general's judgement. Georgia troops raided the home of a family that had always been supportive of the brigade but that also possessed loyalist friends. Seeking a compromise, Marion told the Georgians to return the personal effects that they had taken but to keep any other items. The Georgian officers refused to follow orders. It took the public humiliation of the Georgian troops' captain and the threat of a firing squad to restore order. Even more controversial was Marion's protection of Jeff Butler, a former Tory who was guilty of numerous crimes. Former supporters and valued members of the brigade demanded that Butler hang. When Marion sheltered the renegade in his own tent, the general was both shunned and threatened.

Nowhere was the breakdown of the unit so evident as at Wambaw Bridge on February 24, 1782. A British foraging force caught Marion's regiments, under the command of Peter Horry, unprepared and widely separated.

Marion's two Tory units ran, and the remaining troops fought only briefly. The arrival of Marion, who had been at Jacksonboro with the legislature, accomplished little. He was unable to restore order or to get the commands to work together. Losses were heavy and morale plunged. It was a good thing that the war was almost done because Marion's men were effectively finished.

The war ended in December. Both Tory and patriot soldiers were exhausted, and the colony of South Carolina was on the verge of economic collapse. On December 14, 1782, Greene's army reclaimed Charleston from the British. That same day, Marion summoned his brigade for the last time and spoke to them at Fair Lawn Plantation. He thanked them for their "unwaivered patience and fortitude," and noted that, "No citizens in the world have done more [than] they have." He and Oscar then mounted their horses and rode home to a world destroyed by war.

6. Francis Marion's Last Years, 1783-1795

Even though Marion instructed his men to return to their homes and enjoy "a long continuance of happiness and the Blessings of Peace," there was little at home to which he could return. He was deeply in debt, and he never received payment for his wartime services or reimbursement for the money he had paid to maintain his brigade. His only rewards were a promotion to full colonel in the Continental army and a gold medal. Marion appreciated both honors, but neither provided support. He returned to his plantation at Pond Bluff to find the house burned, his irrigation system destroyed, and no market for the indigo he had always planted. He did not have the means to repair the ravages of war.

Unable to help himself, he continued to serve the people. In 1783, he was on the commission for dividing Charleston District into counties, and in 1790, he was a part of the body designated to draw up a new state constitution. Finally, with the exception of two years, he served in the state senate from 1782 to 1794 at his own expense. As a senator, Francis Marion also led the fight

This is the original manuscript of the South Carolina State Constitution, which Francis Marion helped develop. The constitution was created in 1788 and finally was ratified in 1790.

for free schools, full rights for former Tories, and a stronger militia.

Friends, knowing his debts and realizing that he was too proud to take their aid or public charity, soon came to his assistance. The position of commander of Fort Johnson was created quietly in 1784, and Francis Marion allowed himself to accept the appointment at the salary of $500 a year. In 1786, with the encouragement of his nephew, Theodore S. Marion, and friends, this shy leader of men courted and married his cousin, Mary Elizabeth Videau. On the same day and possibly to convince his uncle to make the move,

This is an engraving of Francis Marion's tomb. It reads, in part: "History will record his worth, and rising generations embalm his memory as one of the most distinguished Patriots and Heroes of the American Revolution; which elevated his native country to Honor and Independence, and secured to her the blessings of Liberty and Peace."

Theodore married Charlotte Ashby. Francis Marion's bride, a wealthy woman, rebuilt the Pond Bluff house and restored the lands. It was here that Marion lived the remainder of his life, dying on February 27, 1795. His tombstone at Belle Isle Plantation, close to that of his brother Gabe, described him best. He was a man who had "the noble and disinterested virtues of the citizen, and the gallant exploits of the soldier; Who lived without fear, and died without reproach."

7. The Legacy

Francis Marion was, in most respects, a typical man of his era. He worked the soil and built his landholdings in the traditional manner by grants and purchases. As the youngest son, he remained with his parents until they died. Being unmarried, Francis moved in with his older brother, Gabe, and helped him raise his family and crops. When Gabe died in 1767, Francis first managed Belle Isle for young Gabriel III, his nephew. Then when Gabriel III died in 1781, his will left the estate in the charge of his uncle Francis. In time Francis Marion delivered the inheritance safely into the hands of Gabriel III's siblings.

It was also typical that as a younger son he sought service in the militia, and, eventually, the provincial army. Without children, Marion could serve in place of his family without endangering their children. Because his land holdings were also slim, it was possible for him to acquire land in exchange for service and one day become a landowner of importance.

What made this shy, quiet, introverted, and unattractive man unusual was his ability to learn from

This is an undated, colored engraving of General Francis Marion by T. B. Welch. It was based on a drawing by J. B. Longacre that was based on a portrait by T. Stothard, who was at the Battle of Eutaw Springs. Marion is in his Continental army uniform and appears to be directing a battle. This scene is romantic rather than historically accurate. In reality, Marion would have been riding his horse in battle.

The legend of Francis Marion is nearly impossible to separate from fact, but Marion's love for and knowledge of the swamps and forests played an important role in the triumph of the Americans. In the 1950s, Marion's homestead was covered by water backed up behind a dam. The lake that bears his name forever covers the priceless heritage of the legendary man called the Swamp Fox.

mistakes—his own and those of others. Although he knew the swamps from his childhood, he was not a born guerilla leader. He observed that hit, run, and surprise were the best tactics for militia, and that good intelligence, superior horses, access to supplies, and a friendly environment made almost undefeatable allies. Thus, with or without weapons, ammunition, or even men, Marion was a threat. British soldiers were so afraid of a surprise attack by the Swamp Fox, that hundreds of enemy soldiers essentially were frozen in place and could not be used elsewhere while the threat of Marion loomed.

Here is a picture of Francis Marion's order book, in which he recorded his daily orders to his men. This is one of the few remaining documents left behind by Marion. He also left a few letters and artifacts that help historians distinguish between the truth about Marion and the countless legends.

In memory of Francis Marion's contributions and his love of the wilderness, a tract of land between the Cooper and Santee Rivers was set aside as the Francis Marion National Forest. These moss-draped trees are part of the Francis Marion National Forest.

Marion's self-sacrifice and ultimate faith in the law and government were also unusual. He gave up everything to the cause of American liberty and never regretted his decision or the loss of almost all of his personal property. When parting with those who had followed him, he was careful to promise that he would "be happy to render them every service in his power" should they at any time need such help. In 1788, former Colonel Hezekiah Maham, fleeing from the law for

This is a photograph of the Stokes Building at Francis Marion University. This is one of the few places where the name of the legendary Swamp Fox lives on in South Carolina.

fraud, solicited Marion's intercession and received it, but only after Maham turned himself in. For Francis Marion, hero or not, the law was the same for everyone.

Today, the Swamp Fox is as elusive as he was during the war. Except for his order books as Moultrie's second in command, a few dozen letters, and limited personal items, nothing remains of the man whose activities intimidated a large part of the British army in South

Carolina. Although many children were named after him in the years following the war, there were no statues, no museums, and no memorials erected in his honor. The Civil War, fought from 1861 to 1865, relegated him to relative obscurity, a situation that the film *The Patriot* (1999), though loosely based on his life, did little to change. All that remain to honor the man and his work are the Francis Marion National Forest, which covers a part of the Williamsburg District, and Francis Marion University in Florence, South Carolina. Although, the author supposes, a man who earned the nickname the Swamp Fox probably would have liked it this way.

Timeline

1732   Francis Marion is born.

1748   Marion goes to sea and is shipwrecked.

1759   Francis Marion serves under Governor William Lyttleton against the Cherokee.

1761   Francis Marion fights with Lieutenant Colonel Grant against the Cherokee.

1763   Francis Marion receives land in St. Johns.

1774   In November, Francis Marion is elected to the General Provincial Congress.

1775   Francis Marion is appointed a captain of the Second South Carolina Regiment.

1776   Fort Sullivan, later Fort Moultrie, is created.

                On June 28, British warships attack and fail to capture Fort Moultrie.

1778   On December 29, Prevost captures Savannah.

1779   On May 11, Prevost almost takes Charleston. Marion leads the defense.

1780   Sir Henry Clinton captures Charleston.

On August 15, Francis Marion closes the
Santee River to British traffic and becomes
commander of the Williamsburg militia.

Between August 20 and October 26, Marion
surprises and defeats the British at Great
Savannah, Blue Savannah, Black Mingo, and
Tearcot Swamp.

Tarleton and his legion chase Marion and his
men through the swamps.

1781 On January 1, Francis Marion's commission
as brigadier general of militia arrives.

Marion establishes Snow Island as a base.

Between March 6–17, Marion traps Major
John Watson in the Black River swamps.

On March 15, Colonel William Doyle raids
and burns the base at Snow Island. The battle at Guilford Courthouse also occurs.

In April, Marion and Lee capture Fort
Watson.

Between May 6–10, Marion and Lee capture
Fort Motte.

In May, Camden, Nelson's Ferry, Granby, and Orangeburg are taken from the British.

On June 5, Marion captures Georgetown.

On July 17, Tory regiments are defeated at Quimby Plantation, south of Biggin Church.

1782

On August 29, Marion surprises the British at Parker's Ferry.

Francis Marion serves as member of the Jacksonboro Legislature.

On December 14, the British troops leave Charleston. Marion disbands his brigade.

1783

On February 26, Marion is given a gold medal for his military service.

On September 30, the Continental Congress designates Francis Marion a full colonel in the Continental army.

1784

1786

Francis Marion commands Fort Johnson.

1790

On April 20, Francis Marion marries Mary Elizabeth Videau.

1795

From May to August, Francis Marion serves on the state constitutional convention.

On February 27, Francis Marion dies.

Glossary

arbitrator (AR-buh-tray-ter) The person who hears a case and determines the outcome.

body servant (BAH-dee SER-vuhnt) A person, often a slave, who takes care of another, often for life.

chagrin (shuh-GRIN) A feeling of embarrassment and annoyance because one has failed.

commissary (KAH-mih-sayr-ee) An army officer in charge of providing an army with food and other supplies.

Continental soldier (kon-tin-EN-tul SOHL-jur) A soldier who was recruited first for one year in 1775 and then for three more, or the duration of the war, in 1776. Continentals were professional soldiers, the equivalent of the British regulars.

countenance (KOWN-tuhn-uhns) A person's face.

court-martial (KORT-mar-shul) A court for the trial of offenses against military law.

derision (dih-RIH-zhen) Ridicule.

disciplinarian (di-suh-pluh-NER-ee-un) A person who believes in enforcing strict discipline.

guerilla (guh-RIL-uh) Any member of a small, defensive force of irregular soldiers.

hostage (HOS-tij) A person who is held prisoner until some demand is met.

Huguenot (HYOO-guh-not) Named for Hugues Basaçon, it was applied to any French Protestant of the sixteenth and seventeeth centuries.

impregnable (im-PREG-nuh-bul) Not capable of being captured or entered by force.

intimidate (in-TIH-muh-dayt) To make timid or afraid.

introvert (IN-troh-vert) An attitude in which a person focuses on his own experiences and feelings; shy.

militia (muh-LIH-shuh) A group of people who are trained and ready to fight in an emergency. In South Carolina, the militia could be called upon for up to two months' service each year.

middling sort (MID-ling SOHRT) Middle class.

naturalize (NA-cher-uh-lyz) To confer the rights of citizenship upon an alien.

obscurity (ob-SKYOOR-uh-tee) Something or someone that is unknown or lacking in fame.

parapet (PAR-uh-pet) A wall or bank used to screen troops from frontal enemy fire, sometimes placed along the top of a rampart.

parish (PAR-ish) An area with its own church and minister or priest.

partnership (PART-ner-ship) When two or more people join together in a business enterprise.

passive (PA-siv) Influenced or acted upon without exerting influence or acting in return; inactive.

petty (PEH-tee) Having a tendency to make much of small matters; small-minded; mean; narrow.

pillage (PIL-ij) The act of plundering or looting.

pound (POWND) English and colonial money, equal to 20 shillings or 100 pennies.

quagmire (KWAG-myr) Wet, boggy ground, yielding under the feet.

redoubt (ri-DOWT) A small fort outside a fortification to defend the gate.

regular (REH-gyuh-lur) A professional soldier.

relocate (ree-LOH-kayt) Move to a new place.

reveler (REH-vuh-ler) Someone who is merry or festive.

Second Continental Congress (SEH-kuhnd kon-tin-EN-tul KON-gres) A body of leaders that was to speak and act for the American colonies from 1775 to 1783. It would help to provide an army and navy, direct the war effort, raise money, and lay the foundation for a new form of government.

solitude (SAH-luh-tood) A lonely place; isolation.

spectator (SPEK-tay-ter) A person who sees or watches something without taking an active part.

stockade (stah-KAYD) A wooden wall made of large strong posts. The posts are put upright in the ground to help protect the area inside the wall.

strategy (STRA-tuh-jee) The science of planning and directing large-scale military operations.

tactics (TAK-tiks) Maneuvering forces into the best position before a battle.

twenty-shilling freeholder (TWEN-tee-shil-ing FREE-hohl-der) A person who owns at least twenty shillings of property and therefore may vote.

Additional Resources

To learn more about Francis Marion and the American Revolution, check out these books and Web sites.

Books

Alden, John R. *A History of the American Revolution.* New York: Alfred A. Knopf, 1969.

Hatley, Tom. *The Dividing Paths: Cherokees and South Carolinians through the Revolutionary Era.* New York: Oxford University Press, 1995.

Rankin, Hugh. *Francis Marion: The Swamp Fox.* New York: Crowell, 1973.

Web Sites

www.earlyamerica.com/portraits/marion.html

www.findagrave.com/pictures/669html

www.lpitr.state.sc.us/marion.htm

www.patriotresource.com/people/marion.html

Bibliography

Garden, Alexander. *Anecdotes of the Revolutionary War in America*. Charleston: A. E. Miller, 1822.

James, William D. *A Sketch of the Life of Brig. Gen. Francis Marion and a History of His Brigade*. Marietta, GA: Continental Book Co., 1948.

Johnson, Joseph. *Traditions and Reminiscences of the American Revolution in the South*. Spartanburg: The Reprint Co., 1972.

Johnson, William. *Sketches of the Life and Correspondence of Nathanael Greene*. 2 vols. Charleston: A. E. Miller, 1822.

Lee, Henry. *Memoirs of the War in the Southern Department of the United States*. New York: University Publishing Co., 1869.

Simms, W. Gilmore. *The Life of Francis Marion*. New York: Derby & Jackson, 1859.

Tarleton, Banastre. *A History of the Campaigns of 1780–1781 in the Southern Provinces of North America*. London: T. Cadell, 1787.

Walsh, Richard. *The Writings of Christopher Gadsden, 1746–1805*. Columbia: USC Press, 1966.

Weems, M. L. *The Life of General Francis Marion*. Philadelphia: J. B. Lippincott, 1884.

Index

About the Author

Louis P. Towles, a native of South Carolina, earned a Ph.D. from the University of South Carolina. He has published *South Carolina Quakes and Shakes*, a history of the state's natural disasters, *A World Turned Upside Down, The Palmers of South Santee*, and numerous articles on local history. Francis Marion has always been a particular interest.

Credits

Photo Credits

Series Design
Laura Murawski

Layout Design
Corinne Jacob

Project Editor
Joanne Randolph

Photo Researcher
Jeffrey Wendt